YOUR VIEW OF ME

YOU LOOK AT MY GENDER

BUT WHAT DO YOU REALLY SEE

MY OUTER APPEARANCE

LONG OR SHORT HAIR

MAYBE AN INTERMEDIATE LENGTH

OR PERHAPS YOU'RE JUST JEALOUS

YOU VIEW ME DIFFERENTLY THAN OTHERS

BECAUSE YOU FOCUS ON IMMATURE MATTERS

PERFECTION IS YOUR ENEMY

BECAUSE YOU NEVER ACHIEVE IT

NOT BECAUSE OF YOUR NATURAL ORIGINALITY

BUT BECAUSE YOU ARE ENVY STRICKEN

TO ME AND MY LOVED ONES

MY OVERALL APPEARANCE IS RIGHT

TO YOU THE JEALOUS; GREEDY ONE

YOU HATE YOURSELF

BECAUSE I AM ORIGINALITY AND CONFIDENCE

BY: LASHUNDRA D. MARTIN (SUI REINYA)

SUI REINYA (Lashundra D. Martin):

Summarized Overall Description

Yes, I currently hold the record

The most kids within a single pregnancy

The most husbands (complete guys) within my

real marriage

The highest ranking female leader

Throughout All Locations

Even Hell And Heaven

And Their Surrounding Locations

THE GREATEST FEMALE WARRIOR LEADER

AMONG MANY OTHERS

YES, I AM A COMPLETE FEMALE

EVERYTHING DOCUMENTED HERE IS

STRAIGHTFORWARD

DON'T WORRY ABOUT IT

NEVER AMERICAN

NO, I'M NOT PERFECT

ALTHOUGH I AM A REAL FRIEND

AND COMPLETELY FAMILY ORIENTED

WITH THREE-HUNDRED PLUS ALREADY ADULT KIDS

SOME ADOPTED AND NATURAL BIRTH KIDS

BIOLOGICAL OR NOT

THEY ARE ALL MINE AND MY CURRENT HUSBANDS

I LOVE THEM ALL EQUALLY LIKE A STANDARD REAL

PARENT

WITH MY LARGE GROUP OF CURRENT ACTUAL

HUSBANDS

TOGETHER, WE OVERSEE IT ALL (MAGICALLY AND

NONE)

WE APPRECIATE EVERYONE THAT HELPS US

Working together towards life, events, celebrations without wrong within it

Professional Entertainment

(Straightforward And Legal)

Our Entertainment Group (Friends And Family)

Organization Leaders (Family And Business)

Worst Than Evil Reputations

(Straightforwardly)

Educated And A Real Team

Now And Everlasting

WITH ALL OF THIS; WHY WOULD I EVER GO AGAINST THEM?

ROYALTY DOCUMENTED (DO YOUR INTERNATIONAL RESEARCH)

BY: LASHUNDRA D. MARTIN (SUI REINYA)

STRAIGHTFORWARD AND CURRENT LEGALIZED LAW ENFORCERS WILL CONFIRM

NO MATTER WHERE YOU LIVE AT; INTERNATIONALLY AND THROUGHOUT IT ALL

FAMILY AND STRAIGHTFORWARD BUSINESS

SOME PEOPLE SAY (FAMILY AND BUSINESS DON'T

MIX)

MAYBE NOT IN AMERICA

AND NOT IN ANY GREEDY; WRONG DOING FAMILY

BUT, YES; IT IS COMPLETELY POSSIBLE

SOME PEOPLE DO RIGHT

WHILE OTHERS LIE TO GET OVER

SOME PEOPLE ARE STRAIGHTFORWARD

WHILE OTHERS BEG AND PLEAD AFTER FAILURE

IT'S NOT ABOUT THE MONEY

IT'S ABOUT BEING TRUSTED

WILL YOU HELP ME BE SUCCESSFUL

OR RUIN MY BUSINESS ON PURPOSE

WAS YOUR PAY RATE TOO LOW OR HIGH

OR DO YOU HAVE HATRED AND STUPIDITY

WHATEVER YOUR PROBLEM IS AND WAS

MY BUSINESS DEALS ARE STRAIGHTFORWARD

LEGAL AND WITHOUT AMERICAN CULTURAL LIVING

NOTHING STUPID, NOTHING CRAZY, NOTHING

SEXUAL RELATED

WHY HURT MY PEOPLE

WHEN WE CAN COME TOGETHER

AND ALL MAKE MORE THAN MULTI-MILLIONS

LIKE STANDARD PROCEDURE

ONLY DOWNGRADERS LIVE FOR THEMSELVES

BY: LASHUNDRA D. MARTIN (SUI REINYA)

SUI REINYA'S ROYAL GETAWAYS REVISED

By: Lashundra D. Martin

ABOUT THE AUTHOR:

I LIKE TO DO CREATIVE PROJECTS FOR FUN/WORK. I LIKE TO HELP PEOPLE THROUGHOUT DIFFERENT LOCATIONS. I STARTED AN ONLINE THERAPEUTIC COMMUNITY; THAT IS FREE AND AVAILABLE TO EVERYONE. I ASKED THAT EVERYTHING POSTED AND ALL MESSAGES BE AS STRAIGHTFORWARD AND APPROPRIATE AS POSSIBLE.

HTTP://SUCCESSFUL4LIFE.PROBOARDS.COM/

SAFE TO VISIT AND FREE

REGISTRATION/PARTICIPATION

THANKS, LASHUNDRA D. MARTIN (SUI REINYA)

TOGETHER WE WILL BE SUCCESSFUL

CREATIVE PROJECTS CAN BE ON ASSORTED SUBJECTS AND IN DIFFERENT CATEGORIES, ACCORDING TO THE ARTIST AND ETC.

PLEASE EMAIL: VALUABLEEXPRESSIONS@GMAIL.COM (ONLY THIS EMAIL ADDRESS)

FOR QUESTIONS, COMMENTS, STRAIGHTFORWARD BUSINESS DETAILS, IMPORTANT MESSAGES, CREATIVE PROJECTS REQUESTS, VOLUNTARY DONATIONS(PAYPAL), AND/OR PAYMENTS (PAYPAL), AND ETC.

Free Online Therapeutic Message Bulletin

Community:

HTTP://SUCCESSFUL4LIFE.PROBOARDS.COM/

Online Events And Tickets:

HTTP://WWW.EVENTBRITE.PT/O/LASHUNDRA-D-MAR

TIN-AND-ADDITIONAL-STRAIGHTFORWARD-EDUCATED

-PEOPLE-8126694421

PROMOTIONAL NAME BRAND ITEMS AND

PRODUCTS:

HTTP://WWW.ZAZZLE.COM/VALUABLE_EXPRESSIONS

+GIFTS

ADDITIONAL WRITING MATERIAL (FOR READERS):

HTTP://WWW.WRITERSCAFE.ORG/SUCCESSFUL4LIFE

FREE ONLINE THERAPEUTIC DISCUSSION:

HTTP://SUCCESSFUL4LIFE.PROBOARDS.COM/BOARD

/1/GENERAL-DISCUSSION

ADDITIONAL LINK WITH UPDATED INFORMATION:

HTTPS://PLUS.GOOGLE.COM/11734040942651672957 2

ONLY THIS EMAIL ADDRESS (FOR CONTACT AND

PAYPAL PAYMENTS):

VALUABLEEXPRESSIONS@GMAIL.COM

RESEARCH LASHUNDRA D. MARTIN (SUI REINYA),

AND/OR L.D. MARTIN ONLINE FOR FUTURISTIC

UPDATES ON THE LATEST

AND YES I AM ALREADY ON THE MAP

EVERYTHING IS SOLD ONLINE

THROUGHOUT ALL LOCATIONS OR WILL BE

EVENTUALLY

MY ALREADY CURRENT ACTUAL HUSBANDS; CAN LOOK ME UP AND FIND ME WITH EASE LIKE STANDARD PROCEDURES. THIS IS COMPLETELY STRAIGHTFORWARD AND REAL INFORMATION; IF I HAD ANYTHING TO DO WITH IT. I ONLY DESIRE TO BE WITH MY OWN CURRENT ACTUAL HUSBANDS; AND THAT'LL NEVER CHANGE, NO MATTER WHAT HAPPENS

LASHUNDRA D. MARTIN (SUI REINYA)

INTERNATIONAL DOCUMENTED LEADER

TOGETHER WE WILL BE SUCCESSFUL

PEOPLE DIE DOING EVERYTHING BY THEMSELVES

(STUPID AND/OR CRAZY)

Everything is originally by Lashundra D.

Martin (Sui Reinya) and I hope you enjoy my

writings

Feel free to visit all of the websites and

internet links listed throughout the book

I look forward towards working with you

and/or sharing additional creative projects.

Thanks, and email me if you have any

questions or comments about my work.

ValuableExpressions@gmail.com

HAVE WE DONE THIS ALREADY

LET'S SEE HERE

WHERE SHOULD WE BEGIN

OH YES, THAT'S RIGHT

WE ALREADY GOT STARTED

HAVE WE ALREADY FINISHED INTRODUCTIONS

IF NOT THEN, I AM SUI REINYA

MY AMERICAN IDENTITY IS LASHUNDRA D. MARTIN

No, I'm not a mixed breed of some sort

Yes, I am a pure foreign female leader

I don't impersonate guys in any way

Although I have played in different movies as

a guy

It was my something different

And my way of staying close to my husbands

I LOVE THEM SO MUCH

I'LL NEVER LEAVE THEM; I KNOW THAT ALREADY

WE HAVE BEEN MARRIED FOR OVER A CENTURY

THAT'S A LONG TIME

BUT NO MATTER THE TIME FRAME AND OUR

CURRENT LOCATIONS

OUR MARRIAGE AND UPLIFTING WAYS OF LIVING IS

EVERLASTING

WITH OUR FAMILY, FRIENDS, AND ADDITIONAL LOVED

ONES

MAYBE YOU'RE SPEECHLESS

AND/OR HAVE YOU NOTICED

I AM MYSELF

STRAIGHTFORWARD

EDUCATED

APART OF A REAL MARRIAGE

FAMILY ORIENTED

ORIGINALITY AND NATURAL STANDARD OVERALL

A Real Friend

Talented

Athletic

Completely In Love And Obsessing With My

Already Husbands

Never Sharing My Husbands

Have Great Work Ethics

Current Leader And Overseer

Et Cetera (Etc)

Need Or Want Some Therapeutic Help:

Do you sometimes feel like expressing things

on your mind?

Do you feel lonely and need someone to talk

too?

Have you ever experienced anything that

causes you to feel left out and emotional?

Are you worried about something or

someone?

ARE YOU EXCITED ABOUT SOMETHING THAT YOU WOULD LIKE TO SHARE WITH THE WORLD?

WOULD YOU AND/OR SOMEONE YOU KNOW LIKE TO REGISTER TO POST AND REPLY TO MESSAGES FROM PEOPLE THROUGHOUT DIFFERENT LOCATIONS WORLDWIDE.

WOULD YOU LIKE TO TELL ADDITIONAL PEOPLE ABOUT THIS LOCATION AND SHARE THINGS WITH EACH OTHER BECAUSE YOU HAVE A HARD TIME KEEPING IN TOUCH (CONTACTING FRIENDS AND FAMILY) OR SOMEONE ELSE?

DO YOU HAVE NEW INFORMATION ABOUT SOMETHING IMPORTANT THAT YOU WOULD LIKE TO SHARE?

WOULD YOU AND ADDITIONAL PEOPLE THROUGHOUT THE WORLD LIKE TO COMMUNICATE ABOUT NEW IDEAS, AND WHATEVER THAT YOU WOULD LIKE TO EXPRESS?

IF SO, THIS IS THE PLACE FOR YOU! JUST REMEMBER TO KEEP IT CLEAN AND STRAIGHTFORWARD INFORMATION AS BEST AS YOU CAN.

THANKS, ANYONE IS WELCOME TO JOIN OUR NEW CHATTING LOCATION OR THERAPEUTIC COMMUNITY. LET THE CHATTING, POSTING, AND SHARING BEGIN!

Contact Information And Payment Options:

If anyone would like some help with creative

projects, jobs, careers, professions, etc

Please email me:

ValuableExpressions@gmail.com

And we can work on whatever that is

straightforward and legal together

AND DISCUSS PAYMENT OPTIONS

DON'T WORRY, EVERYTHING WILL WORK OUT AND

WE CAN BE SUCCESSFUL TOGETHER LIKE A REAL

CARING AND CONSIDERATE TEAM OF CREATIVE

PROFESSIONALS.

LASHUNDRA D. MARTIN (SUI REINYA)

LOOKING TO MAKE INVESTMENTS AND/OR DONATE

FINANCIAL CONTRIBUTIONS

EMAIL ME: VALUABLEEXPRESSIONS@GMAIL.COM

THIS EMAIL IS ALREADY REGISTERED WITH PAYPAL

YOUR STRAIGHTFORWARD AND LEGAL INTERESTS,

IDEALS, PLANS, GOALS, OBJECTIVES, AND/OR ET

CETERA (ETC)

I'M SURE WE CAN ACCOMPLISH STRAIGHTFORWARD

BUSINESS DEALS TOGETHER THAT WILL EVENTUALLY

LEAD TO SUCCESS!

Free Online Therapeutic Community: Message Bulletin Board

I AM A STRAIGHTFORWARD PERSON THAT LIKES TO DO CREATIVE PROJECTS AND HELP PEOPLE THROUGHOUT DIFFERENT LOCATIONS. I PLAN ON SHARING DIFFERENT WRITING MATERIALS/CONTENTS WITH EVERYONE LOOKING FOR SOMETHING NEW, INSPIRATIONAL, FUNNY, EDUCATIONAL, LIFE RELATED SITUATIONS TO HELP ENCOURAGE OTHERS FROM MAKING THESE MISTAKES, AND ETC.

I RECENTLY STARTED A NEW THERAPEUTIC COMMUNITY THAT IS COMPLETELY FREE TO EVERYONE. YOU CAN VIEW, REGISTER/SIGN UP TO POST AND REPLY TO EACH OTHER'S MESSAGES. I ASK THAT EVERYTHING BE STRAIGHTFORWARD INFORMATION AND APPROPRIATE TO KEEP DOWN CONFLICT AND PROBLEMS.

HTTP://SUCCESSFUL4LIFE.PROBOARDS.COM/

PLEASE VISIT THIS MESSAGE FORUM AND FEEL FREE TO EXPRESS YOURSELF, WHERE YOUR WORDS ACTUALLY MATTER!

AND EMAIL ME IF YOU HAVE ANY QUESTIONS, COMMENTS, AND ETC.

THANKS, AND WE CAN WORK TOGETHER ON THE DETAILS, BUSINESS AGREEMENTS, PAYMENT OPTIONS, AND ETC.

I LOOK FORWARD TO WORKING WITH YOU; AND PLEASE, DON'T WAIT UNTIL THE VERY LAST MINUTE.

Introduction And Recognition

Story By: Lashundra D. Martin (Sui Reinya)

Sometimes people hear others talking about doing different things to be successful, and get angry or jealous. Sometimes people want everything to go their way only, and don't care about what additional people feel, think, need, or want in life.

NOW, LETS BE COMPLETELY REALISTIC ABOUT ALL OF THIS. IF EVERY SINGLE PERSON TRIED TO DO EVERY INDIVIDUAL THING OR TASK BY THEMSELVES, HOW WOULD THEY EVER BENEFIT AND/OR PROFIT IN ANY WAY?

NO MATTER WHAT YOU START WITH; YOU WILL EVENTUALLY NEED ADDITIONAL PEOPLE AND MATERIALS; BECAUSE YOU WON'T HAVE ENOUGH TIME/MEASUREMENTS WITHIN ANY GIVEN DAY TO PRODUCE AND MANUFACTURE EVERYTHING NEEDED STANDARD FOR SURVIVAL.

No matter what products or materials you use; everything has to come from somewhere and it goes through at least one procedure before you get the finished product or material.

Some people think ("they got this"), because they're not stupid and they can do any and everything.

YOU MEAN TO TELL BE THAT YOU:

CAN MAKE EVERY SINGLE PIECE OF CLOTHING YOU

LIKE TO WEAR; AND PRODUCE ALL OF THE FOOD YOU

LIKE TO EAT, AND MANUFACTURE ALL OF YOUR

HYGIENE AND ADDITIONAL CLEANING PRODUCTS;

AND MANUFACTURE YOUR ADDITIONAL GROOMING

PRODUCTS; AND PRODUCE AND MANUFACTURE

EVERYTHING NEEDED TO PRODUCE AND

MANUFACTURE BECAUSE YOU HAD TO START WITH

ORIGINAL NATURAL RESOURCES FOUND AND

COMBINED STRAIGHTFORWARDLY AND

APPROPRIATELY WITH EQUAL MEASUREMENTS TO

GET ADDITIONAL RESOURCES NEEDED FOR

STANDARD WAYS OF LIVING; AND TRANSPORT EVERYTHING TO THE LOCATION WHERE YOU HAVE TO COMBINE EVERYTHING IN A CERTAIN WAY (NOT BECAUSE THAT'S WHAT YOU LIKE, BUT IF YOU DON'T COMBINE COMPLETELY RIGHT; YOU WILL BE AUTOMATICALLY SUICIDAL WITHOUT PREVIOUS WARNINGS, AND/OR YOU CAN'T GET WHAT YOU NEED BECAUSE YOU HAVE TO HAVE THIS TO PRODUCE AND MANUFACTURE ADDITIONAL THINGS NEEDED FOR SURVIVAL), AND GET WELL RESTED TO HAVE STRAIGHTFORWARD RESPONSIBLE FUN, ENJOYMENT, EXCITEMENT, PARTIES, CELEBRATIONS, AND ETC; I KNOW YOU DON'T WANT TO CAUSE PROBLEMS

BECAUSE BY NOW IF YOU HAVE LASTED THIS LONG, YOU HAVE ALREADY HAVE ALOT OF PROBLEMS BUILDING UP RELATED TO YOU NEEDING THINGS FOR SURVIVAL.

YOU MEAN TO TELL ME YOU DID ALL OF THAT AND YOU DON'T HAVE WHAT YOU NEED BY NOW. BUT YOU ALL FOR YOU AND YOU ONLY. SO SELF-CENTERED AND ARE YOU STILL TRYING TO FORCE ADDITIONAL PEOPLE TO WHORE AND PROSTITUTE TO YOU, BECAUSE YOU HAVE/HAD LEVERAGES AND ADVANTAGES.

WHAT HAPPENED?

YOU SAID AND HEAVILY ADVERTISED ("YOU DID EVERYTHING BY YOURSELF" AND PUT EMPHASIS ON "EVERYTHING")

NOW YOU'RE CRYING AND WOULD RATHER BE STUPID, CRAZY, AND BLAME GOD/HIS SON, FOR YOUR WRONGFUL ACTIONS (CRIMINAL ACTIVITIES AND/OR SINS)

It was easy to have a large group of straightforward and educated people working standard throughout the year manufacturing and producing all and appropriate materials and products needed standard for your survival.

All you had to do is work with us, help store and transport different materials, keep our straightforward legalized peace agreements between the countries, nations, and all locations.

THE POINT OF THIS IS TO HELP PEOPLE UNDERSTAND THAT IT IS EASIER, MORE STRAIGHTFORWARD, APPROPRIATE, AND WORTHWHILE TO WORK TOGETHER FOR OUR SURVIVAL. SOME PEOPLE TRIED DURING EVERYTHING BY THEMSELVES AND DIED BECAUSE IT'S STUPID, JUST PLAIN CRAZY.

WHY WOULD AMERICANS AND ADDITIONAL PEOPLE BRING THIS UPON THEMSELVES?

I JUST DON'T KNOW!

YOU NEVER HURT, KILL, DEPRIVE, TRY TO CONQUER, AND/OR GO AGAINST A GROUP OF PEOPLE LIKE THAT.

YOU KILL YOURSELF AS A FORM OF PUNISHMENT; BY YOU BEING STUPID. THESE PEOPLE WORKED FOR EVERYONE WITHOUT BEING SELFISH AND GREEDY. THEY NEVER FORCED ANY WRONGFUL ACTIONS OR ACTIVITIES ON YOU (LIKE BEING A SEX SLAVE TO SURVIVE FOR A SLIGHT CHANGE OF THE BARE MINIMUM); BECAUSE YOU NEEDED HELP AND THOUGHT SEXUAL ACTIVITIES COULD BE USED AS A FORM OF PAYMENT.

SEX IS USED TO REPRODUCE FUTURE GENERATIONS.

IN AMERICA AND SOME ADDITIONAL LOCATIONS IT IS

USED TO PASS AROUND SICKNESS AND ILLNESSES,

COMMONLY REFERRED TO (STDs AND CANCER);

WHICH THE ORIGINAL CARRIERS GOT IT FROM THEIR

FAVORITE BAD HABITS OR SOMEONE ELSE'S (SOME

ARE BORN AS CARRIERS BECAUSE THEIR PARENT(S)

HAD/HAS A HISTORY OF PARTICIPATING WITHIN

CONSUMING, DISTRIBUTING, RETAILING, AND ETC;

AMERICANS FAVORITE BAD HABITS (ILLEGAL DRUGS,

ALCOHOLIC BEVERAGES, TOBACCO PRODUCTS, ETC)

EVERYTHING DON'T COME WITH A FINE PRINT AND SOMETIMES THINGS BUILD UP AND SICKENS YOU OVER TIME (GRADUAL TIME FRAME/PERIOD.

DON'T WORRY ABOUT DOWN GRADING PEOPLE, THEY NORMALLY DO STUPID AND CRAZY THINGS THAT EVENTUALLY KILLS THEM ANYWAY.

JUST TRY TO STAY FOCUSED ON STRAIGHTFORWARD

IMPORTANT THINGS IN LIFE, AS BEST AS YOU CAN.

REPORT WRONGFUL ACTIONS MADE AGAINST YOU,

ESPECIALLY THINGS THAT ARE LIFE-THREATENING

AND DANGEROUS; WHENEVER YOU CAN WITHOUT

CONSISTENTLY COMPLAINING ABOUT THE SAME

THING, IF YOU CAN HELP IT. AND IF THINGS

PROGRESS AND BECOME WORSE, TRY REPORTING TO

A DIFFERENT LOCATION, A HIGHER DIVISION, ETC

IT'S NOT GUARANTEED TO SAVE YOU; HOWEVER, IT WILL BE DOCUMENTED AND YOUR DEATH WON'T BE IN VAIN, ESPECIALLY IF YOU NEVER DESERVED IT.

THE PEOPLE RESPONSIBLE WILL EVENTUALLY RECEIVE PUNISHMENT ACCORDINGLY, SOMETHING WILL BACKFIRE OR COME BACK ON THEM, OR THEY WILL MEET THEIR MAKER (GOD/THE DEVIL) SOMETHING WILL HAPPEN TO THEM AS A FORM OF PUNISHMENT GUARANTEED, ESPECIALLY IF YOU NEVER DESERVED IT.

My advice to you is try to live a straightforward way of living without establishing a bad reputation. Because no one wants a leader that whores and/or prostitutes. Straightforward business never had anything to do with sexual activities of any kind; because your financial situation will remain the same, unless you're losing out this one time to slander someone else's trustworthy reputation, and then that person and everything/ everyone that person is apart of and have been apart of.

SOMETIMES THINGS MIGHT GET SOMEWHAT

CHALLENGING, HARD, DIFFICULT

EVERYONE APART OF OUR STRAIGHTFORWARD

SURVIVAL TEAM PROBABLY HAS EXPERIENCED

SOMETHING AND ENDURED SOME THINGS THEY

NEVER EXPECTED AND/OR WANTED ALREADY.

AND OUR EXPERIENCES MOTIVATED US TO WORK

TOGETHER LIKE A REAL FAMILY OF INDIVIDUAL

LEADERS; TOWARDS SURVIVAL WITH OUR OWN

DESIRED, UPLIFTING, EXCITING, WAYS OF LIVING.

TOGETHER WE ARE SUCCESSFUL, NUMEROUS, AND

FREE AS OURSELVES. AND THERE'S NOTHING WRONG

WITH IT, NO MATTER WHERE WE ARE INDIVIDUALLY

AND/OR AS A TEAM.

LIVE YOUR OWN LIFE AND STOP TRYING TO FORCE OTHERS TO BE YOU. BECAUSE EVERYONE WAS MADE TO BE THEMSELVES. AND WHAT YOU ARE TRYING TO DO IS IMPOSSIBLE; THAT WILL EVENTUALLY LEAD YOU TO YOUR OWN DESTRUCTION/DEMISE.

PEOPLE IMPERSONATING OTHERS WILL FORGET WHO THEY ARE, CONSTANTLY SWITCHING PERSONALITIES, PLAYING CARTOON CHARACTERS, AND BUILDING FALSE IMAGES/REPUTATIONS.

EMAIL ME FOR QUESTIONS AND COMMENTS IF

NEEDED:

VALUABLEEXPRESSIONS@GMAIL.COM

LASHUNDRA D. MARTIN (SUI REINYA)

INTERNATIONAL DOCUMENTED LEADER

TOGETHER WE WILL BE SUCCESSFUL

PEOPLE DIE DOING EVERYTHING BY THEMSELVES

(STUPID AND/OR CRAZY)

Lashundra D. Martin And Additional

Straightforward Educated People

HTTP://WWW.EVENTBRITE.PT/O/LASHUNDRA-D-MAR

TIN-AND-ADDITIONAL-STRAIGHTFORWARD-EDUCATED

-PEOPLE-8126694421

MY AMERICAN NAME IS:

LASHUNDRA D. MARTIN

I AM A STRAIGHTFORWARD EDUCATED PERSON THAT

LIKES TO HELP PEOPLE THROUGHOUT ALL

LOCATIONS.

I WOULD LIKE TO HELP BRING PEOPLE TOGETHER TO

DO FUN AND EXCITING THINGS WITH CLOSE FRIENDS,

FAMILY MEMBERS, BUSINESS ASSOCIATES, AND

ADDITIONAL STRAIGHTFORWARD EDUCATED PEOPLE;

SEARCHING FOR PEOPLE WHO ARE LOVING AND

CARING.

SOMETIMES IT SEEMS LIKE, NO MATTER HOW LONG

AND HARD I WORK, I AM NOT ABLE TO HELP

EVERYONE THAT IS EXPERIENCING FINANCIAL

HARDSHIPS, LONELINESS, EMOTIONAL DISTRESS

FROM LACK OF FAMILY SUPPORT, AND ADDITIONAL

THINGS THAT WILL BE IMPROVED FROM US WORKING

TOGETHER TO HELP THEM.

COMING TOGETHER AS STRONG SUPPORTIVE GROUPS, TEAMS, BUSINESSES, ORGANIZATIONS, FRIENDS, FAMILY AND ADDITIONAL STRAIGHTFORWARD CATEGORIES; WE CAN MAKE COMPLETELY POSITIVE AND EXTREME CHANGES IN PEOPLE'S LIVES LOOKING TO MAKE IMPROVEMENTS AND IN NEED OF SUPPORT FROM SOMEONE WHO CARES, IS COMPLETELY STRAIGHTFORWARD, NOT DANGEROUS, AND NOT SOMEONE LOOKING TO USE AND MISTREAT PEOPLE, NO MATTER THEIR SITUATION.

I KNOW I AM NOT ABLE TO DO EVERYTHING ALL MYSELF; WHICH IS WHY I WANTED TO PUT TOGETHER SOME LEGAL AND STRAIGHTFORWARD IDEAS OF MY OWN AND COMBINE THEM WITH THE HELP AND SUPPORT OF ADDITIONAL PEOPLE THROUGHOUT ALL LOCATIONS.

I AM ASKING PEOPLE THROUGHOUT ALL LOCATIONS; WILL YOU PLEASE HELP ME, TO HELP ALL IN NEED OF HELP, IN SOME FIXABLE WAY, LEGALLY AND WITHOUT DISCRIMINATION?

IF I EVER GET A CHANCE TO REWARD EVERYONE
THAT HELPS ME, I WILL. PLEASE KEEP A RECORD OF
EVERYTHING YOU PURCHASE AND OF ALL OF YOUR
DONATIONS TO MATCH UP WITH THE GOVERNMENT
AND MY OWN.

I THANK EVERYONE FOR THEIR SUPPORT AND THEIR
CONTRIBUTIONS TO MY EVENTS AND ADDITIONAL
THINGS THROUGHOUT OUR LIVES.

I LOOK FORWARD TO MEETING AS MANY PEOPLE AS
POSSIBLE AND HELPING PEOPLE THAT WILL LIKE TO
RECEIVE OUR HELP.

AND JUST IN CASE YOU WERE INTERESTED IN SOME ADDITIONAL PRODUCTS THAT ARE CATEGORIZED TO BE NAME BRAND PRODUCTS AND SOMETHING DIFFERENT; VISIT THE ONLINE STORE VALUABLE EXPRESSIONS PARTNERED WITH ZAZZLE, AND SEARCH FOR LASHUNDRA D MARTIN OR L D MARTIN TO VIEW AND/OR PURCHASE NAME BRAND PRODUCTS.

CLICK ON THE URL OR WEBSITE AT THE TOP UNDER

THE HEADING/ TITLE ON THIS PAGE. THE ONE

UNDERNEATH IS JUST A REMINDER, JUST IN CASE

YOU WANTED TO WRITE IT DOWN.

HTTP://WWW.ZAZZLE.COM/VALUABLE_EXPRESSIONS*

REMEMBER TO ZAZZLE BABY

IT'S A NEW SLOGAN, NO OFFENSE INTENDED

YOU CAN ALSO ENTER "LASHUNDRA D. MARTIN OR

L.D. MARTIN" ONLINE WITHIN THE ZAZZLE

COMPANY TO VIEW CURRENT NAME BRAND

PRODUCTS AND ITEMS AVAILABLE FOR SALE.

HTTP://WWW.ZAZZLE.COM/VALUABLE_EXPRESSIONS

+GIFTS

THE ZAZZLE COMPANY HAS ALOT OF SALES

THROUGHOUT THE YEAR

AND YOU CAN VISIT LASHUNDRA D MARTIN'S FACEBOOK PAGE FOR ADDITIONAL INFORMATION ON CURRENT EVENTS AND SOME EXAMPLE NAME BRAND PRODUCTS.

THANKS

IS LASHUNDRA D MARTIN REALLY PREGNANT; BECAUSE SHE HAS HAD A LOT OF TROUBLE EATING WITHOUT GETTING SICK. DID MIKE CONLEY, LEBRON JAMES, KOBE BRYANT, OR SOMEONE ELSE IMPREGNATED HER? AND HOW WILL THE STRAIGHTFORWARD EDUCATED CURRENT FAMILY MEMBERS OF THE ROYAL FAMILIES HANDLE THIS SITUATION? I HAVE TO KNOW, FIND OUT UP CLOSE, AND IN PERSON; ASAP, PLEASE.

SUI REINYA'S IMPORTANT MESSAGE

This Email Address Only:
ValuableExpressions@gmail.com
(PAYPAL APP)

By: Lashundra D. Martin

HTTP://WWW.EVENTBRITE.PT/O/LASHUNDRA-D-MAR

TIN-AND-ADDITIONAL-STRAIGHTFORWARD-EDUCATED

-PEOPLE-8126694421

HTTP://WWW.ZAZZLE.COM/VALUABLE_EXPRESSIONS

+GIFTS

HTTP://WWW.WRITERSCAFE.ORG/SUCCESSFUL4LIFE

HTTP://SUCCESSFUL4LIFE.PROBOARDS.COM/BOARD

/1/GENERAL-DISCUSSION

HTTPS://PLUS.GOOGLE.COM/11734040942651 67

29572

THIS EMAIL ADDRESS ONLY:

VALUABLEEXPRESSIONS@GMAIL.COM

BUSINESS NAME: VALUABLE EXPRESSIONS

(PAYPAL)

LIGHT TURQUOISE (SKY BLUE AND A LITTLE GREEN

MIXED) BACKGROUND

MATCHUP THE IMAGE ON THE NEXT PAGE

SUI REINYA'S VALUED EXPRESSIONS:

Poetry Among Other Things

By: Lashundra D. Martin

RECEIPT MESSAGE: LASHUNDRA D. MARTIN (SUI REINYA);

THANKS, TOGETHER WE WILL BE SUCCESSFUL

RESEARCH LASHUNDRA D. MARTIN, SUÍ REINYA, AND/OR L.D. MARTIN

ONLINE FOR FUTURISTIC UPDATES ON THE LATEST

(CURRENT ACTUAL HUSBANDS)

AND CURRENT MAILING ADDRESS ONLY

EVERYTHING IS SOLD ONLINE

INTERNET AND/OR ONLINE RESEARCH:

LASHUNDRA D. MARTIN (SUI REINYA)

ON GOOGLE MAP FOR DRIVING DIRECTIONS